TWO BEARS
at the seaside

Story by Cathie and David Bell

Pictures by Jan Brychta

Oxford University Press

For Emily

Oxford University Press, Walton Street, Oxford OX2 6DP

Oxford   New York   Toronto
Delhi   Bombay   Calcutta   Madras   Karachi
Petaling Jaya   Singapore   Hong Kong   Tokyo
Nairobi   Dar es Salaam   Cape Town
Melbourne   Auckland

and associated companies in
Berlin   Ibadan

Oxford is a trade mark of Oxford University Press

© Oxford University Press 1990
Printed in Hong Kong

A CIP catalogue record for this book is available from the
British Library.

The Two Bears Books are:

Two Bears at the seaside
Two Bears in the snow
Two Bears at the party
Two Bears go fishing
Two Bears find a pet
Two Bears and the fireworks

One day in the middle of summer,
Stanley and Winston woke up very early.
The birds were singing in the trees,
and the sky was clear and blue.

Winston and Stanley wanted to go to the sea.
Winston went to the cupboard and took out
his purple swimming trunks and a pair
of sunglasses.

Stanley sorted out all the things
they needed for the trip:
buckets, spades, towels, sun hats,
and an umbrella in case it rained.

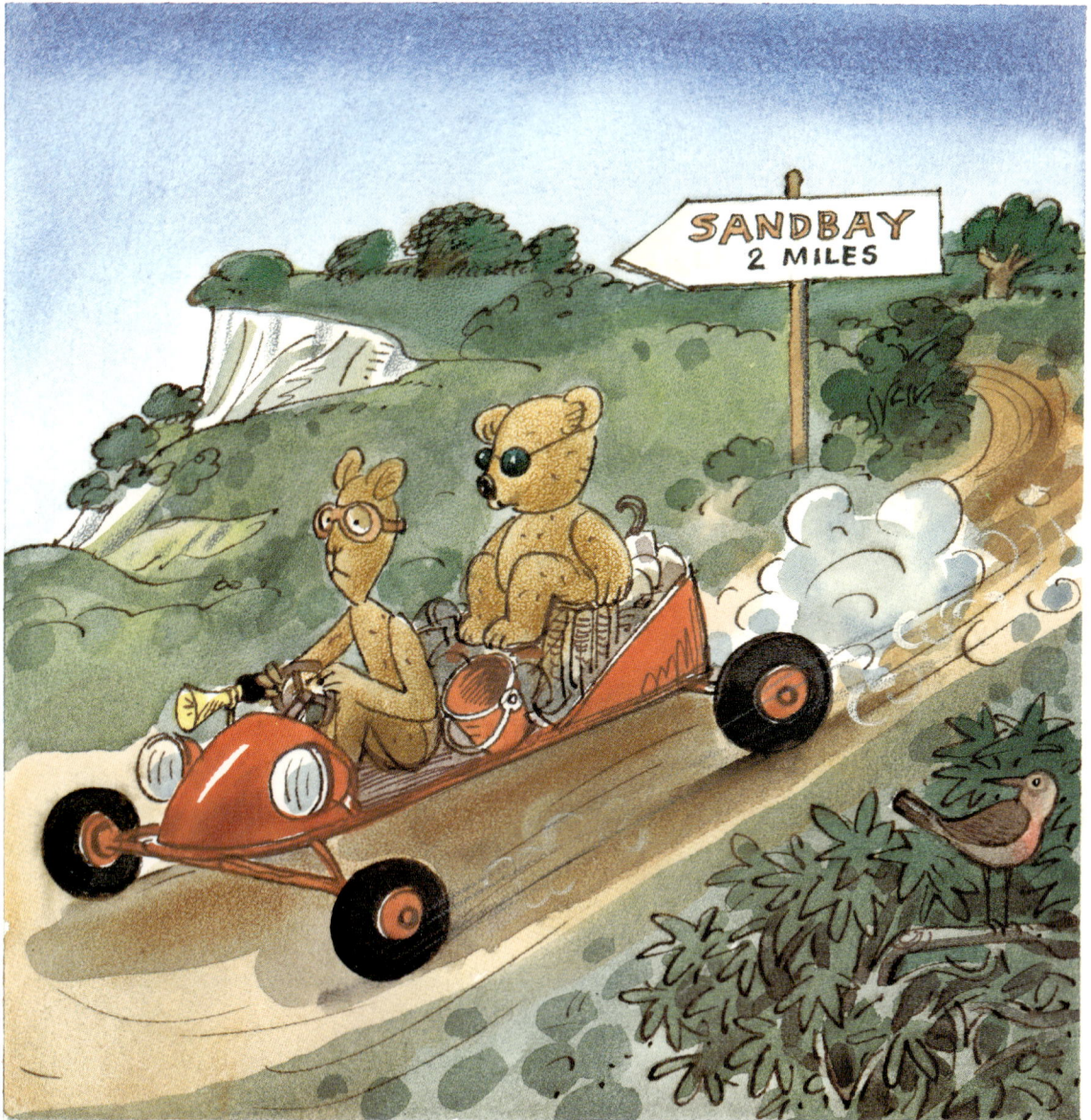

They put everything into the go-kart.
Stanley drove and Winston sat on top of the things.
It was a long way to the sea. It was hard work going
up hills but it was good fun going down hills.

When they arrived at the seaside, they were very hot.
They bought ice-creams to cool down.

Winston saw a poster about a sandcastle competition.
'That sounds fun!' he said, 'I'd like to do that.'
He filled in an entry form.

The sun was very bright. Winston put on his sunglasses.
'I wish I had a pair of sunglasses,' said Stanley.
'Why don't you go for a swim,' said Winston, 'and
I will build my sandcastle.'

Stanley went for a swim. He swam around for a
long time. He put his head under the water and
saw a crab and lots of fish.

When Stanley came out of the water there were
sandcastles everywhere.
'I wonder if Winston has finished his sandcastle?'
said Stanley.

But Winston was fast asleep!
'Oh no,' said Stanley. 'The judges will be here soon.
I'll build the sandcastle myself.'

He dug a moat and put all the sand into the middle.
He put lots of towers around the edge of the castle.
He made a bridge, and a road, and little windows
made from shells.

The judges came round and woke Winston up.
'Your castle is the best we've ever seen,' said the
judges, 'you win first prize.'
Winston was very surprised.

They gave Winston a big badge and a prize.
Winston gave the prize to Stanley.
'It's your castle, so it's your prize,' he said.

Stanley opened the prize. It was a wonderful
pair of sunglasses.
'Just what I wanted,' he said.